W9-AUI-148

Unspeakable ShaXXXspeares